Home at Last

W0006879

Poems by Leslie Stewart

ISBN: 978-0-9783995-8-0

Editor: Dorrie Murdoch

To purchase additional copies contact :
>Leslie Stewart
>831 Cambridge Road, RR 2,
>Montague , PE C0A 1R0
>(902) 962-3918

Publisher:
>Wood Island Prints
>670 Trans-Canada Highway, RR 1
>Belle River, PE C0A 1B0
>(902) 962-3335 schultz@pei.sympatico.ca

Printing:
>Lightning Source Inc. (US)
>1246 Heil Quaker Blvd.
>La Vergne, TN 37086 USA
>Voice: (615 213-5815
>Email: inquiry@lightningsource.com
>www.lightningsource.com

Thanks for financial support by *Southern Kings Arts Council*

A special thanks to my children and grandchildren, and to my wife Dorrie, for their good-natured and enthusiastic involvement in this volume.

Table of Contents

Little Waves

The waves that are washing
Upon our island shore
Have these waves been here before?

Do they know the sand of our shore?
When one comes, they always bring more
These little waves have traveled so many miles
Watching them play and splash, they bring a smile

The waves wash and roll back again
They remind us of old lost friends
The salty spray fills the air, with a down-home smell
Come and play they say we have stories to tell

The little waves so much fun for play
That's why people come here for their holidays
The waves laugh at Mom and Dad
It's the most fun they have had

The waves bring us gifts from a far
It could be a lobster trap or a jar
We find old driftwood washed upon the shore
From an old boat, a dock, there's always more

The waves that are washing
Upon our island shore
Have these waves been here before?

We find seaweed, stones, nets and shells
Mussels and sometimes an old fish that smells
There are always lots of foot prints in the sand
The waves try to wash some away if they can

I once went away to another island
And watched a wave washing that sand
In the warm Caribbean ocean water warm
Back home frozen bays and snowstorms

I asked a wave as it washed ashore
Have you been to Panmure Island before?
It didn't reply and washed away
Will I see that wave, another day?

Catch a Cloud

Have you ever laid on your back
While watching clouds wander by?
They change shape and size, making
New things way up in the sky

Some are little skinny lines of
White pale feathers floating along
Others remain large dark and billowing
Thundering and singing a song

The horizon remains covered with
Low marshmallow clouds of light grey
The wind will blow hard at times
Trying to make them go away

Between white caps of thundering waves,
The blue of the sky is hidden from me
As now I lay on the beach sands
On my soft belly looking out to sea

I tried running along fast as can be
With my little legs, then jumping in the air
The clouds hang so close to the ground
Yet I've never caught one, but I don't care

After all what would one do with it?
When caught do you make it a pet
A big fluffy cloud either fat or thin
What if a rain cloud? Then you'll all be wet

No, clouds are best left all alone
Drifting by way up in the sky
So now just take it easy and enjoy
Those wonderful clouds drifting by

Grandchildren Come To Stay

When our grandchildren come to stay
No matter the weather, it's a wonderful day
Ours come to see us from far away
When they come by car it takes days

They once flew down for a holiday
Emily and Alice were first to stay
Then Maple brought her parents one day
Yes, these are little girls that come to stay

But in the future a grandson will stay
When we open our door on that special day
Little voices will echo we've come a long way
So grandpa let's go to the ocean and play

We can find snails and shells buried in clay
Grandma and us, found spitting clams one day
And once we used the sand dunes to sleigh
No matter what they say or do in a day

It's always too short of an island holiday
So sad to see them leave and go away
We know they'll be back another day
Grandchildren are our children in yesterday
It's just we look at them a different way

Their grandfather

Little Butterfly

I'm a little butterfly
Look at me
Don't my wings
Look so lovely

Brightly coloured
In shades of green
The most beautiful
Insect you have seen

My wings are big
My body is small
I love all flowers
Love them all

We come in all
Colors, shapes and sizes
See us as we
Fill the skies

Some of us fly
To Mexico
They don't like it
In the snow

You can dress
And look like me
The most beautiful
Butterfly they'll see

Drifting Along

I'm going to go
Up in the sky
Learn to float
As a Butterfly

Watching the flowers
As I drift by
Way up high
In the skies

Lift my wings
Gently glide by
All those flowers
In the countryside

I'll settle down
On a Daisy plant
Share my lunch
With some ants

Black-eyed Susans
Catch my eye
Bright yellow petals
I see from the sky

Purple coneflowers
Prick my feet
But the nectar
Is good to eat

I'm not a moth
But a butterfly
See my wings
As I drift by

Beautiful designs
On my wings
Painted by an artist
A beautiful thing

I'd be happiest
As a butterfly
Floating by
Up in the sky

Landing on flowers
Pretty one I see
I'd be happier
Than a bumble bee

A rainbow of color
As we drift by
Millions of us
Lovely butterflies

Floating along
In the summertime
This wonderful life
A dream of mine

Lost

I don't know where I'm coming from

I don't know where I've been

I don't know where I was going to

I don't know if I'll go back again

Lizard Lost

I lose my lizard
In a snow blizzard
It was an iguana
I don't know what it wanna

It go out in the snow
Where it go I don't know
Didn't have a toque or hat
Snowshoes, mittens and that

It brings tears to my eyes
It could freeze and die
Lost this stormy day
My lizard run away

Maybe it go next door
It gone there before
It go in the winter time
That pet iguana of mine

To lie around the fireplace
My iguana has good taste
They cook it on a stick
And that was the end of it

Where You Bee

Bumble Bee, Bumble Bee
Where can you be?
I don't want to be
Stung picking flowers
For mommy and me

Bumble Bee, Bumble Bee
Don't mistake me
For some enemy
Don't sting my hand
I'm your little friend

Bumble Bee, Bumble Bee
I hear you humming
Do you see me?
I'm only picking flowers
For mommy and me

Rock and Roll Baby

It's dark and gloomy
As we sailed from
Our safe red shore
Dad, Me and Mom

I was laid upon
The slippery bow
My father went forth
The waves he ploughed

I bounced and rolled
Up and back and forth
Further out to sea we went
Our heading due north

White caps of waves
Watered me down
If I roll off the bow
I'll never be found

No time to stop
And turn around
I'd be a goner
Sink and drown

A crazy spot to be
Lay a baby there
One good wave
I'd bounce in the air

Scooped up by an eagle
In those claws no doubt
A defenceless baby
Being tossed about

If not an eagle
Gull or a crow
I'll be fish bait
That I know

As I lay on the bow
Of my parents' boat
I had given up
There being any hope

Moms are marvellous
As you all know
Watching their children
As they grow

As for me this day
The future looks small
Fall off this boat
No future for me at all

The sun is rising up
Daylight I see
Morning is broken
Can they see me?

Rock and Roll Baby

I again bounce
Rock and roll
Where we are
I don't know

Finally my mother
Lets out a scream
I was mislaid
So it now seems

Where's the baby?
She yells at Dad
I don't know where
Him, I never had

You had him, I know
Wrapped in a sheet
I remember you
Laid him at my feet

No you had him
By the bucket of bait
Where is the bucket now?
Find it before I faint

I see the bucket
No baby inside
I was on the bow
Going for a ride

Ten miles from shore
Now! They look around
For that tiny baby
Not to be found

Looked through the cabin
And boxes below
Hey! Look on the bow
I'm here you know

I can't speak
Or even yell
I'm a helpless baby
Can't you tell?

The boat is now stopped
They're sick inside
Thinking I was gone
Fell off and died

It was up to me
To signal a sign
I muster all my gas
Let it go out my behind

This was the signal
That led them to me
Abandoned on the bow
Their little baby Leslie

Mothers

Where would we be without our mothers?
Some of us wouldn't have sisters and brothers
My father wouldn't have had his wife
As for me, I would have missed a chance at life

Lots we can say about mothers and love
They must have received their guidance from above
How could she know so much about life?
And my dad always said 'he had the best wife'

She frowned when that doctor spanked you to cry
Mothers feed us from the first twinkle in our eyes
She held you close to her, proud as can be
You were her special gift, for the family to see

Mothers dress us, feed us, and put us to bed at night
Mother would say "love your sister don't fight"
When my older brothers were teasing me
I always ran for safety onto Mother's knee

When you awoke in the morning, your mother was there
No doubt in the kitchen making breakfast with care
When you came home for soup and sandwich at lunch
She spat on a hankie to wipe your face as you munched

My mother the nurse applied bandages at will
To cuts and bruises, then made us take awful pills
When I was sick and lay fevered in my bed
Mother read a story and put a cool cloth on my head

Mothers tell us to go to school, learn the golden rule
Life will be hard enough as it is, no point in being a fool
Mothers help with homework,spelling, math, geography
Somehow she knew it all, smart as only teacher could be

Mothers wash all our clothes, dishes, floors and you and me
Must have thought I was a dirty floor, she scrubbed endlessly
Mother would wash our hair; soap everywhere, in ears and eyes
Rinse our heads under the tap, or a cold bucket, now don't cry

Mothers mend our shirts and pants, lose a sock or two
They may shrink a sweater we don't like, we say, "thank you"
My friends always said my mom was the best mom around
She could be serious, demanding,strict, forgiving, or a clown

Mothers never let us wander too far from the home
On our trykes, bikes, going by car, remember to phone
We are fastened by a magic string only mothers pull
There is a gentle tug every now and then just to let you know

Mothers

Our mothers work hard and long with very little pay
So buy her a special gift of love, on this her mother's day
If you don't have your mother any more, she has passed away
Then the greatest gift is to remember her with love and say,

"I love you Mom, happy Mother's day!"

Island Mother

I raised my boys from babies
What great fathers they've become
I know it was my doing, maybe
Whatever, it sure was lots of fun

I remember cleaning those babies' bums
And sometimes the pee would fly
If I had girls instead of island sons
Lay them on their back and not get it in the eye

I would use a clothespin, just to make it dry
I know it never hurt them, yet they would wail
It was well worth it, not getting peed in the eye
And I feel much better, after telling of this tale

I would dress them as girls, those island boys
Dresses of pink, some of yellow-dots and apricot
They never had trucks or tractors for toys
But earrings, lipstick and dresses they got

These are my island sons raised by me
Their father was a farmer and fisherman too
He was often out in the fields or off to sea
Not around much, to see how they grew

The boys got to drinking their father's beer
He made it in the backwoods far from the house
I would say the Lord's not happy and put in the fear
They often came home with red mud, on their blouse

All was fine by me until the day school started
I wished he was a girl, not a boy in that dress
Because when he got nervous, he twitched and farted
By the time the bus cleared, what a mess

School became a happy place for the boys
Each one started much the same as the last.
They slowly dropped their dresses and girlish toys
Now it's all tucked away in their childhood past

It's not easy being a mother on lonely P.E.I.
You wish for some things that never come
Thinking about my girlish boys, brings a tear to my eye
To have had a daughter, as one of those island sons

Day dreaming

I was dreaming of a better time
Oh, a different life you see.
If I could only find that damned genie
Three wishes she could give to me.

I would wish of traveling, maybe in the sun
Get that golden tan; go on the beach for a run.
Instead back to the clothes line, another sheet to hang
The sink is full of dishes, now the telephone rang.

Can somebody answer that call, I'm busy
Father sleeping on the couch, oh is he?
The vacuum quit working, the washer on the blink
And now I see more beer bottles, covering the sink.

I would wish for the finest clothes fit for a queen
Jewels of diamonds, gold, emeralds so green
It's the ball diamond and rings around the collar
Hey Julie, it's supper time, give your brother a holler.

Their clothes are too small or just worn out
Wake up your father give him a shout.
Dinner is made, now food is on their plate
In twenty seconds their food they will have ate.

I would wish the man I married, ten years or so ago,
Still looked handsome, tall and thin you know.
I must be doing the washing wrong, the ironing at that
I see his shirts have shrunk; his pants are short and fat.

Yes my life has become quite busy, raising all these kids
I've had the nine children, so ask what he did.
He was just a fisherman, spent his lazy time at sea
No wonder folks say, "The children all look like me".

Yes, I was dreaming of a better time.
Maybe a different life for me
But this is the only place I would want to be.
My family and the man that fishes from the sea

Young Love

Down by the river
The water does flow
I meant this tiny bird
And he told me so

Two young people
Came down today
They made love
Rolling in the hay

One of the parents
Came walking by
Both of them kids
They tried to hide

She saw them in
That field of hay
They caught hell
For being that way

Now she'll be
An unwed mom
Just for have-in
A little bit of fun

He'll run off
Never come back
That old farm boy
His name was Jack

Her name is little
Mary Anne Jane
And for her
Life will never
Be the same

Want for a Wife

I don't know what on earth
She's doing with a guy like him
He is tall and wiry as can be
Some homely looking guy, Jim

His hair is awful, if that
Is hair, it's battleship grey
I'm sure on those misty
Cloudy days he fades away

He would be a hard man
To find working in the fog
I have my doubts you
Couldn't find him with a dog

The fish smell he permeates
Will bring lobsters to shore
The best use of a lobster trap is
To keep him from her door

She can do a whole lot better
Take a good-looking man like me
We're the same age and all
And I've worked all my life at sea

No fish smells permeating
From the pores of my skin
I weigh over three hundred pounds
I'm a man, not the likes of him

If wedding bells were to chime
It would be best, for her and I
I'm the man to see she does right
Not that sorry-ass-looking guy

I can't imagine the scene
On their wedding night
She would have to show him
What to do; he's not that bright

I would carry my lovely bride
In my arms, across the threshold
Place her ever so gently on the bed
Then go and dress in my robe

It would be the best surprise
For her, on our wedding night
That a fat-ass man, I could make
Love to her, from dusk to light

On this wildest of wedding nights
Let it truly and proudly be said
That we wore those brass legs
Right off that old honeymoon bed

Just at that precise, lovely moment
He got a slap across the head
By his mother, as he was dreaming
About taking his brother's gal to bed

"Get off your fat ass and get down
To the wharf and help with the rig
Go help your skinny-ass brother
Fix that old broken thing-a-ma-jig"

Sitting and Waiting

I was just sitting here, spending my time
Waiting for you, because I didn't mind
Was it to be eight o'clock or nine?
I know you weren't listening but that's fine

Because it's well past ten now don't you see?
I thought you said you loved me"
Maybe I'll just sit here; I don't mind, it's fun
Twelve passed by, now it's one

Sitting and waiting for you
My bum is some sore, just passed two
Your watch doesn't work I see
Mine, well it just passed three

It looks like the day is coming alive
The church bells chimed, now it's five
Sure missed that dinner I needed some
Seven more times the bells have rung

My stomach is starting to ache
I see it's half past eight
Well eight went by so fast
Soon you will be here at last

I may have closed one eye or two
Whatever, I must have missed you
I'll wait another hour or so
Because I really miss you
Just thought you would like to know

Memories of Mine

Back long ago, when I was young,
We wandered field and far.
Many island tunes we sung,
With our fiddle and guitar

Our bodies tanned from summer sun
The joy of laughter and tears
When we were young all was fun
On this island we love so dear.

We fiddled and riddled and rhymed
And danced to a grand old time

Watching fishing boats bob in the bay
Reflecting waters of time
Old fishermen tanned as island clay
These are memories of mine

Tunes in our heads, rhythm in our feet
And love in our hearts
That when my love and I did meet
And never will we part.

We still feel the music and riddle and rhyme
Now we sit on old rocking chairs
And watch the young folks dance in time
As joy and laughter fill the air

We fiddled and riddled and rhymed
And danced to a grand old time

Wife Shopping

At Eighty-Three, he thought about a wife
To have a companion that would be nice
He had never married nor had a girlfriend
He had milked the cows and worked the land

Always too busy, way too much work to be done
Life for him only hard work, no time for fun
That has changed, time to find himself a wife
Time to share the work, for the rest of his life

Lots of time left until he is One Hundred Three
Twenty years with a woman, a good life it should be
How was he going to find one? Where would he look?
The first place he thought, was in the phone book

Under *headings* he took a look for, *Wanted a Wife*
The closest he found, were the words *Wildlife*
He looked again, this time he found *Marriage*
Now this looked promising, partners in old age

You could get *Counselling Service and Family Support*
Better than he hoped, a wife, children none to report
Never been with a woman, so no children he said
When he gets married, it will be his first time in bed

Maybe if he went to town, that's Charlottetown
Check out some women and take a look around
This was worse than he thought it might have been
The only older women he saw were in their sixties it
seemed

Where were the older ladies he was interested in?
Harder work than he thought it should have been
He went over to the other big town of Summerside
Thought a lot about his future during the ride

Around the streets, up blocks and down lanes
This search was looking pretty much the same
Where in the hell were the women his age keeping?
Maybe, just maybe they'd all be at home a' sleeping

They save their energy for dancing all night
He'd never done such things, now he just might
After all he had now just turned Eighty-Three
And a new exciting life he wanted it to be

He stopped for a coffee, a nice chance to unwind
Asked the waitress where some women he could find
He was looking for a wife to be, in her late Seventies
Had travelled to both towns and none he had seen

The lady laughed and gave out such a great roar
You will have to look in a senior citizens store
They're living together, as bees do in a hive
Hoping this way they might all stay alive

The shopping should be easy for a man like you
You have your own teeth and a new pickup too
Lots of gals might take you up on that historic ride
To go live in an old farm house and be your bride

Do your laundry, dishes, and sweep the floor
Milk the cows, plough the fields and more
She would save her strength for going to bed
I feel sorry for you, the first woman you said

He was uncertain just what she meant by that
He was in good shape, had a little belly fat
He stopped in to shop at a senior citizens home
"Welcome" it said "You'll never be home alone"

Pickin's was slimmer than he could have dreamed
All the women in walkers or wheelchairs it seems
Nothing healthy looking here, he could call a wife
It was warm inside true, but a pitiful way of life

The quest was done, he headed back for home
His pickup was empty of a wife, he was alone
He washes his own dishes and cooks a great meal
Always did his laundry and the land he did till

Ploughed the fields, fed the herd, and milked the cows
It was during the milking that night he thought "wow"
This was as close as he would come to having a wife
His hands had been on the best teats all his life

Leslie Stewart: Home at Last

Good Times Or Hard Times

I'm dreaming of my family and island home
They're all I have and love so faraway.
I'm working in the oilfields out in Alberta,
Digging on this cold god-awful November day.

Only to be digging for clams or fishing at sea,
Or walking with my wife holding her hand.
Instead I'm breaking this frozen ground,
With pick and hammer, working the land.

They said this was to be the Promised Land
The west was the place I should be.
Money flowed and jobs they were plenty
They said it was like taking kelp from the sea.

Now I live with my good buddy
And five hundred more like me.
We came searching for our future
That is back home fishing in the sea.

No jobs on the island for men like us.
Where are farmers, fishermen, and carpenters by trade?
Times are sorry poor, no money and debts to the sky.
We left our wives, children, parents and friends we made.

The small towns are getting even smaller
Some villages are gone, no one seems to care.
Country roads and lanes aren't traveled anymore
Cars sit empty, tractors rest in lonely fields of despair.

I'll take a rest and sit on this frozen old stump
The forests here have much in common with the sea.
They change colour and rise and roll forever
Snow rests on their tops, as breaking waves would be.

So it's back to work and swing that heavy hammer,
I'm breaking up the ground, another road to repair.
Tom from Kinross yells to Robert from Murray River,
"Did you see that dog last night"? "That's no dog, it's a bear".

Now that sent a chill from my backside to my head
Never saw a bear before, but I've seen a whale or two.
Funny how my mind works, it always takes me back home.
It hurts me now inside, because I'm thinking of you.

We have music here at the camp, some men do the jig.
One guy plays the spoons and fiddlers we have a few.
Two guys play the banjo, another dozen can sing
This old guy from Cambridge, he tells a joke or two.

Most of us have travelled by boat, truck or rail,
Just to get here in Alberta, before the heavy snow.
There will be no homesick here, for here you have to stay
When spring is around the corner, then home we will go.

I see the Rocky Mountains, way off in the distance.
Dark grey and blue, with ragged tops and round.
They remind me of a summer storm on the Island.
Clouds rise and bank together, then the rain comes down.

The days are getting longer, the sun is warming up.
I'll be able to sleep in my long johns soon.
I wear my parka all day and heavy blankets at night.
I am a little nervous with five hundred men in a room.

Old Walter Dixon, heard a train the other day.
He said the whistle sounded like the ferry at Wood Islands.
Calling us to be ready to board, soon time to go home
We all laughed and smiled to the very last man.

The road was finally done and there was the corner
Spring had come at last: time to head back east.
Some men had already left, others waited for their last pay
I was glad to be heading back home, just to say the least.

As we traveled back home by rail, the ship of the land
We islanders became young children at play.
It was much like waiting at Christmas, under the tree.
Time to open our presents and we'll be home to stay.

The roads are still dusty, times are still sorry poor.
We brought home some hope and we pay the bills.
My tractor ploughs a field to plant some potatoes
We all hope that hard times are over and say it's God's will.

I made new friends while working out west
Some live around the corner, others far away.
My wife is going to have another baby
So it's good times or hard times, home I'll stay.

Leslie Stewart: Home at Last

I Lost My Boat, On St. Mary's Bay

I lost my boat, on St. Mary's Bay
The sad sight still haunts me today
She was my dream, hand built by me
Crafted over the winter, I worked endlessly

Cutting, gluing, sanding with care
Finger joints, dovetails, lots of hardware
Brass screws, stainless and four-inch nails
I had her name on my mind, I knew it well

I was an island boy, but now a man
No need for those blue print plans
I've known that bay all my time
Watched the tides come and go, I'll be fine

I've worked on mussel boats
Lobster boats, anything that floats
Spring was coming on fast
I knew winter wouldn't last

The ice was melting on the bay
Yes, soon it would be my day
I'm not a dreamer, I'm a man
I've build that boat the best I can

Got some special paint for dorys
Mine was bigger than that, sorry
This was a real ship, a man o' war
Built for adventure, high seas and more

I painted her sunset orange and red
Sharp looking craft my friend said
It was now mid April, the ice melted away
Yes, very soon it would be my day

The name was hand painted by me
She was now ready for the sea
Life jacket? not for this seaman
I will not bob in the bay, swim I can

Onto the bay, the water was ice blue
The water is a little cold, it will do
Off I go, as many a sailor before me
With a mighty stroke, set off to sea

A little water started to come in
Maybe the glue had been a little thin
I gave it no real need for worry
This was my day, I was in a hurry

Now the dory paint is looking really good.
Maybe I shouldn't have used some new wood
The old outhouse walls, they'll float you know
I had asked the Home Lumber guy, he said so

Finally I was out there, on St. Mary's Bay
A lot of water was coming in the boat, not ok
The water lapped over the gunnels
I had forgotten the bucket, couldn't bail

It was soon time to abandon ship
Springing overboard, slipped a disk
I saw my dream ship sink that day
If only a life jacket, to bob in the bay

The stern rose out of St. Mary's Bay
There, with her proud name on display
I knew it was a gesture of goodby
And that brought tears to my eyes

She was my good ship, I called her the E.I.
There will never be another like her, bye
Employment Insurance had built that ship for me
It had funded my ship that sank in the sea

I lost my ship on St. Mary's Bay
I hope when your ship comes in today
You will spend your fortune a different way
Than to have your ship sink in St. Mary's Bay

A Distinguished Man from Tignish

A distinguished old man
From the Town of Tignish
A man of many adventures
To be like him, I wish

He must have travelled
The world by sea and sail
To have ventured so young
Go and give the world hell

I see in his deep blue eyes
The reflection of the sea
They show a mystic time
A wild lad, must have been he

Hoisting sails to catch the winds
To take him beyond the shores
Travel to so many exotic places
He'd never been to before

A distinguished-looking man
Always dresses in light grey
He taps his smoking pipe
As hot ashes blow away

The pipe tobacco of Old Dutch
Gives off a fragrance of time
It takes him back to long ago
To wonderful memories in his mind

When he was at sea, so long ago
New lands passed before his eyes
Did he ever think of his home
In Tignish, and wonder why?

The magnet of the high seas
It took him from his town
To sail the world all over
Great adventures he found

His friends from school days
All young lads brave as he
They all stayed at their homes
Not to sail like him the high seas

They worked their family farms
Caught lobsters and raked Irish moss
Saw sunrises and loved the sunsets
Staying at home for them wasn't a loss

A distinguished humorous man
Tells us stories hard to believe
Of working on rum schooners
In the warm Caribbean sea

Chasing pods of Killer Whales
Off the west shores of B.C.
Surfing the Great Barrier Reef
Mermaids he has claimed to see

Outran pirates off the African shore
Smuggled illegal contraband
Rum, tobacco, guns and more
Making a living, a time so grand

He tells of being shipwrecked
On an island just south of Spain
Most of the crew had perished
Only five of them did remain

He says this with a twinkle
In his eye, just to let you know
That this is just a tall tale
The truth may not be so

A distinguished likeable man
He's from the Town of Tignish
Raised on the wild high seas
To be a man like him, I wish

Leslie Stewart: Home at Last

Bizarre

Isn't it strange?
Isn't it bizarre?
How we came
To where we are

I was born up
In old Ontario
Came to the island
One I didn't know

In what direction
How could I know?
Some fifty years later
Where I would go

I read some books
The story of Anne
How she was an orphan
Of Prince Edward Island

Little did I know?
But here I am
Living down here
On that island

I'm not an orphan
A small girl like Anne
Heck no! I've come here
As a crabby old man

Father of three
Grandfather of four
And I'm sure soon
There will be more

But as for now
It's ok by me
To be a grandfather
Living by the sea

Isn't it strange?
Isn't it bizarre?
How we came
To where we are

Iles de la Madeleine

I've come to this island
Surrounded by the sea
What is the name of it?
Please tell it to me

Prince Edward Island
You have come to see
The home of Confederation
They tell this to me

It used to be French
But that didn't last
Now that it is English
The French drive past

They have their own island
Further out into the sea
They take a car ferry
From the town of Souris

They call it the
Iles de la Madeleine
These islands are smaller
To them I have never been

You can take that ferry
From the town of Souris
Go to the Madeleines
Those are surrounded by the sea

You can take your car
That you have driven in
When you get there
Drive around the Madeleines

You'll be further out to sea
Than I have ever been
As I have never left
Prince Edward Island

I love this, my home
The birthplace of me
I don't want to leave
My island, you see

People come to visit my island
They come here from away
From all over the world
They come here to stay

Sexy, Fit and Slim

I want to be fit
I want to be thin
I want to be sexy
I go to the GYM

I run on the treadmill
I sweat a great deal
I race on the stationary bike
I know what I must look like

A crazed mother of three
Won't some guy look at me?
I got a nice tight little bum
Five minute abs, I have some

I look my best in blue jeans
My strutting is some mean
I practice my walk alright
To catch a husband I might

I use my body as bait
So I can get a good date
I'm looking for a guy with money
Who'd love to be with this honey

My three girls need a rich dad
Be the fourth husband I've had
I enjoy the chasing in life
I'm not a very good wife

That won't deter what I do
Spend my time looking for you
They find it hard, all the men
Not to stare at me when they can

Travel the Island I will
In search of the best deal
There might be another rich man
Hungry on Prince Edward Island

I want to be fit
I want to be thin
I want to be sexy
I'm trying to catch him

Gotta Ride

Island Cowgirls
Riding the range
Rustling the boys
Playing their game

All leathered up
Wearing chaps and hat
My Cowgirl outfit
Worth looking at

Riding my stallion
All day long
On the island
Singing my song

Yippy I Ai
Yippy I O
Island Cowgirls
Ride'em so

Riding my stallion
Using my knees
Making him sweat
Showing no mercy

Digging my spurs
In his side
Island Cowgirls
Gotta ride

Roping those steers
Throwing them down
Handling the boys
On the ground

Making my mark
Branding those steers
Letting them know
Who's boss here

Yippy I Ai
Yippy I O
Island Cowgirls
Ride'em so

Gotta Ride

Cowgirl by Choice

The clock radio begins to play
Announcing the start of my day
A great country tune fills the air
I'm waking up without a care

I'm alive let the day begin
I can hardly wait to see him
My man he's already awake
Up at sunrise for goodness sake

I'll make my own breakfast
As I have in mornings past
Fresh cut fruit, some yogurt alright
Fresh orange juice, toast done light

The summer sunlight fills the room
Dancing on the knife, fork and spoon
The warmth of the rays tickles my skin
I begin to smile, just thinking of him

Make my coffee, and then sit outside
Marvel at the beautiful countryside
The rolling hills, spring fed stream
I have chosen the best place it seems

A male blue bird serenades me
Singing so sweetly from his tree
Ha there's that brown rabbit
One with a very, very bad habit

He eats the tops off my lettuce
I'm growing them to feed us
Finish my coffee, and then off I go
Ah, just got bit by a mosquito

That's a warning make no mistake
Rub on plenty of bug screen, all it takes
With this outfit, I look like Daisy May
Heading to the barn to throw some hay

I hear the horses as they kick about
They know I'm late again to let them out
It is a most gorgeous summer morning
As I saunter my way without warning

The half door is open for fresh air
Just our way of showing we care
Unhook the screen door swing it wide
Take my first peek at them inside

The faces have turned looking my way
Their mouths open whinnying to say
Where have you been until now?
Why we're so hungry for our chow

The first horse is my old Missy mare
A beautiful old gal with golden hair
My first horse given to me by my Dad
As I rub her soft nose I feel so glad

She was my horse from the get go
I used to ride her at the horse shows
Sometimes we'd get a ribbon prize
She is old now, so we don't ride

Beside Missy making all the fuss
Is my other horse that lives with us
Willie, the name of my handsome man
The best quarter horse on the island

A chestnut brown, beautiful to ride
Nice, smooth, long floating strides
I have fallen asleep on him at times
Riding through the forest in springtime

He has never let me down, my man
He knows, as I rub his coat with my hand
It's the love and respect for each other
I have not found this love in another

Yes this is my man, love of my life
Oh I'm married and a good wife
Don't take me wrong in what I say
It's just I love my horses better, ok?

The Cat From Away

The cat from away
Found us on a Sunday
We were sitting at home
I was on the deck alone

I didn't see her, when she arrived
It was some time just after five
I was drinking my beer
When she first appeared

At first there was a soft meow
Then she landed on my lap, I yelled
With this startling fear
I spilled some of my beer

There we sat eyeball to whisker
I was afraid to yell, so I whispered
Dorrie, Dorrie come and see
This strange cat sitting on me

Dorrie came out onto the deck
Took a look, what the heck?
Who is your new friend, Leslie?
Was is it a he or is it a she?

It was too early in our relationship
The cat's claws now stuck in my hip
It seemed content, and then she purred
She was a grey cat with white fur

This is why I knew she was from away
Her fur was white, not pink from island clay
She seemed to be a friendly cat
Not too skinny and not that fat

Dorrie said I should give her a pet
I was nervous and said, "Not yet"
She became quit content, and settled down
With claws now in my stomach, she looked around

May as well drink the rest of my beer
With this strange cat, sitting on me here
I had been looking out onto St Peters Bay
When visited by this cat from away

No doubt she was lost, lost from where
She must have a family, some one who cares
No name tag or collar on the cat
She was content, lying on my fat

I gave her a gentle touch of my hand
With a soft purr, we were now friends
Slowly her claws began to retract
I shifted in my chair, not to hurt my back

Where did she come from, I say,
This grey and white cat from away
Lost from a cottage or a home
Abandon from a car to roam

Now Dorrie was more gentle than I
She picked up the cat, I didn't cry
Some claws were still stuck in my fat
I wasn't bleeding, thankful for that

With some warm milk for a treat
The cat came back to sit on my feet
Maybe her owner was a man
She liked me, as her new friend

We placed signs of lost cat found
Hoping that someone from around
Had lost their cat, or someone they knew
As we have their cat, to give back to you

Summer came and turned into fall
We still have the cat; no one called
She's not as white as she used to be
Rolling in the clay down by the sea

We have giving up on finding her that home
She has adopted us, not far does she roam
We have a special affection for this cat from away
And are blessed with us she came here to stay

Barney

Oh there Barney fat cat
How did you get like that?
Eating caviar, must be nice
With young birds and mice

Is it high on cholesterol?
Eating mice and all
Fancy dish I must say
Having a mouse a day

You don't eat bird nest soup
Eat the whole family in a swoop
The parents have wings to fly
You patiently wait as they go by

If you were light and thinner
The parents could be your dinner
I see you use the bird bath well
It's full of feathers, do tell

Do you teach the birds to swim?
Just before you swallow them
Do you wash your paws and face?
Does it wash away the birdie taste?

I see you like to play with your meal
Flipping the mouse is the big deal
Can you double size that to go?
Two fat mice are better crunching slow

The crows and ravens you would try
If someone baked them in a pie
As it is they're the same size as you
Do they think of you as cat stew?

Maybe better to work as a team
They eat birds and mice it seems
Maybe best to collaborate
Or for dinner you'll be ate

Like a lion in the African plain
Our backyard is your domain
I see the red-tailed hawk up high
Hear him call as he glides by

You're too heavy a meal for him
He would only check you out if thin
I knew all that weight would come in handy
Other wise you would become cat candy

I don't mean to pick on your weight
When I fill your dish you can't wait
Munching and crunching you eat like that
You must be feeding the other eight cats

Oh Barney fat cat you do alright
You're safe inside the house at night
When the sun come up out you go
With your fat belly hanging so low

We love you Barney in spite of what I say
We look forward to seeing you each day
It's the birds and mice that have to worry
Here comes Barney, you better hurry.

Sassy, Black Cat

Hey, little black cat, what do you say?
Lying there on the floor this sunny day
You should be outside chasing a mouse
Not lying around in this warm house.

I know that it's cold, it's winter outside.
You've got that black fur covering your hide.
You should be out in that brisk fresh air
They say it's really good, for a cat's hair.

I think you are dreaming of a warmer day.
It's under the old woodstove that you lay.
Look out the window; see the little birds at play,
Eating seeds, bread crumbs, on this cold day.

Even the mice are outside, going for a sleigh ride
They only have hats and mittens to cover their hides
They're all having fun, in the cold sun
Playing catch me, catch me as they run.

Your friend the raven sits on the house
Waiting for his bread treats, he doesn't like mouse.
So inside you lay on this cold winter day.
While outside, some friends are safely at play.

Oh, I forgot it's your brother they fear,
When he is outside, they never come near.
So where is he now on this cold day?
Oh beside you I see, as you both lay.

So little black cat, the life you have is the best,
You lay around all day, having a rest.
I know mouse meat is not your dining style
And eating bird feathers never brought a smile.

So lay around the house, getting treats
Dorrie throws them close to your feet.
A spoiled Sassy black cat you have become,
Very much loved by us and everyone.

Popcorn

Popping the popcorn
Pop, Pop, Pop

Watching the kernels
Hop, Hop, Hop

We love popcorn
Hot, Hot, Hot

Popping the popcorn
Pop, Hop, Hot

Mmmm Buttery

Be a Pick-Up

Bin, bin
It's a bin
You should
Put your
Garbage in

Don't throw it
On the ground
The wind
Will take it
Blow it around

Wiser to
Put it in
A garbage bag
Container
Or bin

Leave it
In your rig
In a garbage
Bag or in a
Thing-a-ma-jig

Hold that cup
In your hand
Walk a little
Further to a
Garbage can

Buy the paper
Read the news
Give it to a
Friend they
Can use

Empty bottles
You can refund
Pick them up
When you
Walk or run

Fast food
Cartons found
People just
Throw them
On the ground

P.E.I. has its
Own intentions,
Personal
Environmental
Intervention

Myers are the
Recyclable guys
They pick up
The garbage
On P.E.I.

Panmure Island

Down to the sandy beach
To walk the salty shore
I'll take my lovely girl friend
The only girl I adore

I don't need a bottle
Of rum or cheap wine
To keep my spirits up
I have a sweetheart of mine

We stroll on the romantic shore
Catching sparkles in our eyes
Bright loving fireworks
To light up the night skies

The warm island winds
Wash over us, damping our skin
We stroll together as one
Making loving memories within

How fortunate we have become
To find harmony and romance
That bonds my love to hers
I wish others this amazing chance

A stroll on Panmure beach
The sky of brightly lit stars
As the two of us walk together
Forgetting where we are

Panmure Island

There's a Lot

There's a lot
I could do.
I could do
A lot more

I could buy
Some groceries,
Or go to
The pharmacy

I could wash
The windows
What a pain!
Don't you know?

I could run
The vacuum
Around some
Of the rooms

Do the laundry
Wash and dry
I could hang
The clothes outside

I could wash up
Some plates
But the glasses
Will have to wait

There's a lot
I could do
I could do
A lot more

I could clean
Around the sink
Take out the
Garbage that stinks

I could go and
Get the mail
It would only be
Bills, I can tell

I could pay
One or two
Then what
Would she do?

I'll sit down
Watch T.V.
All this work
Is tiring me

There's a lot
I should do
But I'll leave
It all up to you

There's a Lot

Visit Wee Anne

I've heard of this wee girl Anne
Who lives in a faraway land
On an island out in the sea
Much the same way as me

My island is called Ireland
Hers is Prince Edward Island
Mine is the green emerald isle
Where all the "Little People" smile

I'll save up my money I will
And work very, very hard until
I've got me money for the ticket
Oh this trip will be some wicked

Looking forward to seeing this Anne
I've read every book of hers I can
How she was an orphan and left alone
Had to go and live at a stranger's home

She must be of Irish blood with that red hair
With it done in braids and freckles everywhere
Only Irish girls could so sparkle and shine
Her adventures are similar to mine

I'm looking forward to speaking to Anne
Go down to Cavendish, walk in the sand
Climb to the top and jump off a sand dune
Sit around a camp fire singing old tunes

I don't have much use for that Gilbert lad
He comes across too smooth, I think he's bad
Anne should keep a watchful eye on him
Young men, you don't know what they're fixin'

I'll have to take that young man aside
Give him a talking to when I arrive
Oh I'm looking so forward to my trip
Just hope now that I don't get sea sick

It's a wreck of a boat I find myself in
I'm cheap with the money, luxury is a sin
It's just as easy to throw up over the rail
As it is to lie in my bed doing it in a pail

Nothing like a drink of whisky to settle me down
I'm sleeping near the engine room, cheapest found
I don't mind the fumes and the engine knocking
What's making me sick is all that bloody rocking

They say we'll be in Rustico in a day or two
This old tug leaking water, swim I may have to
Finally the red soil that I've heard so much about
I'm happy for two things, that I'll give a shout

Here at last safe on shore, standing on dry land
This is beautiful, Anne's Prince Edward Island
Up the shore to find that house with green gables
Can't believe I'm here resting at a picnic table

In a short time I'll be seeing my island Anne
Don't forget I've got some words for her man
It's a nice farm they're living on here today
In the books I've read, it doesn't look this way

I think my dream has burst, more of a nightmare
Look at all these foreign people standing here
They say I've got to pay to go in and visit Anne
I've travelled all this way, best pay what I can

I'm more confused, don't know what to say
There's no doubt I'll need a wee drink today
For there in her hat and long braided hair
In her lovely green dress standing there

Was my hero, the one the only, my Anne
The problem with it, she looks like a man
My good god, this is the ugliest girl that I see
I'm looking and I'm looking, I don't believe

I've travelled all this way, for a picture with Anne
I don't care at this point if she, he is a man
It's for the life of me I don't understand
How Anne of Green Gables is really a man

Turkey Dinner

We've got the potatoes
For the stew
As for the turkey
You will do

We've got sauerkraut
It's the turkey
We're without

Mom has made us
Pumpkin Pete pies
It's you I want
Turkey thighs

Dad got his moonshine
Best liquor out
For turkey dine

But it's you
The turkey
We can't find

Be a good sport
Come for dinner you
We'll make a place
And a pot of stew

Hot sauce and bread
Turkey you will be
Well fed

It's thanksgiving
Time did you know?
And we just want
To show

Islanders can give
And take
Its turkey we want
Make no mistake

Turkey Dinner

Pumpkin Pete

My name is Pumpkin Pete
It's me people love to eat
I make a marvelous pie
Have some, give me a try

When the leaves turn to red
It's this time I'm mostly fed
To thousands world wide
I fill hungry tummies inside

Some prefer whipped cream on top
Fresh from the oven, they can't stop
Others use ice cream, causing me to chill
Warm in a microwave, I taste better still

Mothers make me into big pies
Little children learn and try
They bake the smaller ones
Baking Pumpkin Pete pies with mom

Little Piggy

This little piggy
Went to market
That little piggy
Stayed home

This little piggy
Went to market
Then to everyone's
Home

Bacon and pork roast
Sausage and chops
Hot dogs and baloney
Pig tail treats

The little piggy
That went to market
Food for us
To eat

Snow Job

Long will it be remembered
The great cover-up of 2009

March break had come and gone
Spring was here everyone knew

Good people of Montague
Went to bed not seeing this crime

Overnight they lost their green lawns
In the morning snow covered them
And they were now gone

The Perfect Husband

Yes, the pull cord man
Pull the cord on demand
The perfect husband is he
Pull the cord and you'll see

Do I look lovely tonight?
"Yes you are a beautiful sight"
Do I have the best figure?
"Oh yes" He would deliver

Does this dress suit me?
"Oh it does," answers he
Are my pies the best around?
"No others have been found"

Is my homemade soup a delight?
"Yes they're my favourite alright"
My mother is coming to stay
"I'm looking forward," he would say

Oh I need another diamond or two
"Why not buy more? They suit you"
I'm bored, whatever can I do?
"You're not boring" He would say to you

The pull cord man as a date
Place him in a chair, he waits
And doesn't watch the bar T.V.
He sits, looking at you with envy

Other ladies may walk by
He never moves his eyes
Fixated only upon you
No other date could do

Pull his cord for a reply
He'll never tell you a lie
Honesty is his middle name
Never, never does he play games

The perfect husband is he
The very best he can be
To love you and hold you tight
Pull his cord, he'll say it right

You'll be the envy of all your friends
To have with you the perfect man
They may want to pull his cord too
But remember, he's only for you

Christmas Dream

I had this Christmas dream
Of a perfect husband to be
He would be quite gentle, tall
And handsome looking is he

Never would he talk back
He would only agree
No matter the topic
He always agrees with me

If I need money for clothes
Or my hair done tonight
He is full of compliments
Oh honey, you're beautiful alright

Never would he discuss my size
I could eat all the chocolate cake
Have some fries, fast food burgers
He'd love me, not mention my weight

I could sleep in without reproach
Stay in my warm bed all day
He would have my coffee ready
Breakfast in bed, he would say

The wood stove radiating a glow
He would cover my poor cold feet
Have some Irish coffee with cake
I could cuddle on the couch to sleep

When mother would come to stay
For a short couple of months or two
He would be the happiest husband
I was his wife and he'd thank you

We would travel, a holiday in the sun
I would lie on the warm Caribbean sand
He would bring my favourite drinks to me
My body massaged, by his soft hands

A moonlight stroll along the shore
A cool breeze, he'd hold me tight
Whisper the most wonderful tales
Foolish to resist, his love that night

I'm up having my morning coffee that's hot
Still in a tizzy, about my Christmas dream
And my house is cold, no fire in the stove
I'm not married to him yet, so it seems

I won't give up my dreamy quest
To have the perfect husband in hand
There are plenty of good men on P.E.I.
I'm only after one good Christmas man

About the Author

Leslie Stewart grew up in Ontario, in the small tourist town of Southampton, on the shore of Lake Huron. His life in Ontario and PEI have similarities. He had the beaches of soft white sand, the mouth of a river flowing into the lake, an island just a mile off shore, and the sun setting into the water horizon every night. Yet, here he is living on PEI. Where some things are the same, others are so different—it is the difference that holds him here, warms him, and brings that smirk to his smile. It is also the adventures and making of friends that will continue to anchor him to the shores of PEI.

LaVergne, TN USA
21 April 2010
180082LV00001B/15/P